2Trade 2 Smart

High probability / Low risk strategies

Technical Analysis for any market

Dana DeCecco
Former Commodity Trading Advisor and 15 year independent trader.

Dana has authored hundreds of published financial articles. He maintains four websites dedicated to basic and advanced trading skills.

Lakeside21.com

Copyright © 2012 Dana DeCecco

All rights reserved.

ISBN-13:978-0615734644
ISBN-10:0615734642

PREFACE

This book is a brief and "to the point" advisory about trading techniques and principles that I have found to be reliable. I have tried to explain these concepts using illustrations and examples. I hope you find it informative and helpful.

The chart examples provided are the most recent set-ups that I spent very little time finding. These are common trade set ups that happen every day. I did not search for perfect charts to impress the reader.

Technical analysis is subject to interpretation. This skill can be developed through experience. My goal is to give the reader a jump start at trading. I spent years and years trying to figure out what to look for.

The best trading systems are based on simple rules. I have tried to simplify the trading process and emphasize essential trading techniques. If you are a novice trader, this book will save you years of research.

DISCLAIMER

Trading futures, forex, stocks, and options involves the risk of loss. Please consider carefully whether futures, forex, stocks, or options are appropriate to your financial situation. Only risk capital should be used when trading. Investors could lose more than their original investment. You must review the customer account agreement prior to establishing an account. Past results are not indicative of future results. The risk of loss in trading can be substantial, carefully consider the inherent risks of such an investment in light of your financial condition. The author is not affiliated with any brokers, people, or companies mentioned. Opinions expressed by the author are by no means a solicitation of any kind.

CONTENTS

1. Limited Risk Trading
2. Analysis
3. Charting
4. Indicators
5. Trends, S&R
6. Fibonacci
7. Orders
8. Money Management
9. Make the trade

ACKNOWLEDGMENTS

FOR CHARTS AND VISUAL AIDS

Oanda Forex
IBFX Forex
Free Stock Charts.com
OptionsXpress
MetaTrader MT-4
FXCM forex
StockCharts.com
Interactive Brokers

FOR RESEARCH ON PATTERN RECOGNITION

Larry Pesavento
Scott Carney
H.M. Gartley

DEVELOPER OF THE ZUP INDICATOR

Eugeni Neumoin

A brief note to the reader:

Contrary to popular belief, sharing trading knowledge and systems strengthens the market and enhances your trading system. The more traders using your system, the better it works. Out of all those who read this book only a very small percentage will employ my tactics. Most traders lose money because they are not willing to work at it.

1 Limited Risk Trading

In today's volatile and manipulated markets a limited risk trading strategy is essential. Computer program trading accounts for a very large percentage of market volume. Hedge funds, trading syndicates, market makers, and central banks are some of the players involved in price manipulation.

Stocks, commodities, and currencies are all subject to these overwhelming market forces. Many price movements make no practical sense at all. Program trading is out of control. All participants are not on the same page, resulting in erratic price movements.

According to HL Camp&Co more than 60% of volume on an average day is program trading. This kind of computer based buying and selling can account for 90% of the volume on some days.

It is difficult to determine the directional bias of the program traders. All computer programs must adhere to a set of rules. Technical analysis is the only way to discover the intentions of these programs, when the market will move and in what direction.

Fundamental analysis, news, and reports can be deceiving, unreliable, and manipulative. The only reliable source of information is provided by charting applications. We can believe what we see on the chart. The price chart is history. We can determine the probability of future events through the analysis of historical charts.

Reversal trading has been considered risky and unreliable by many traders. My research concludes that trading market reversals results in high probability trades. Risk aversion tactics are easily employed due to the very nature of the expected pivot point.

Reversal trading offers better entry and exit signals. Upon entering a reversal position, the trader will quickly find out if he is right or wrong in his analysis. If wrong, the trade can be exited with a small loss. If right, the trade is in the direction of the trend with a very early entry.

Market reversals occur in all markets and in all time frames for a variety or reasons. Overbought and oversold conditions are a result of supply and demand. Fundamental economic conditions may account for the general market sentiment. Weather and political events can impact commodities.

Many of these factors can be anticipated and factored into the trading system. All of these factors must be considered when developing a low risk approach to trading the markets. Your money is at risk at all times during a trade.

Computer programs adhere to a set of rules developed by humans. Since unknown future events cannot be programmed into a computer, historical events must be used as a guide. The historical events are recorded on the price chart and can provide insight toward probable future price moves.

Other market forces are at work on the price chart. These forces are not easy to comprehend but they are quantifiable and can be programmed.

These forces are known as Fibonacci levels. They exist on every chart and in every time frame, 100% of the time. The nature of this force is beyond my comprehension but I can see it and I can chart it. It has been referred to as a "market correction". This particular market force is not a historical event. It is an anticipated future event and could be considered a leading indicator.

Most indicators are lagging price movement. There are a few leading indicators at our disposal. If we can chart these effectively we can greatly enhance the probability of a winning trade.

Support and resistance levels are historical price pivot points. Where price has reversed in the past may hold clues to future reversal levels. Trend lines and moving averages are other forms of quantifiable information that can be programmed into a computer.

Trading is a game of probabilities. We must determine the odds of a winning trade before initiating a position. We can get the odds in our favor by employing technical analysis. The charting techniques covered in this book are the best tools available in their predictive ability.

Trading is also a game of risk aversion. Avoiding risk is the prime objective of the market trader. There are many risk aversion tactics available to the professional trader. The focus of this book is to provide simple low risk trading opportunities that anyone can use.

The novice trader can improve trading skills by employing the tactics and methods covered in this brief publication. I have also included a dynamic trading system that can be implemented by anyone willing to put in the time.

This kind of trading makes no sense at all. It is totally idiotic to think that investors are this confused.

Developing a limited risk trading strategy is the best defense in a volatile market. The ability to trade different asset classes provides the trader an opportunity to move on to more stable markets.

This book describes a technical trading strategy that applies to any market that can be electronically traded. This includes, but not limited to stocks, options, futures, and forex. There are a number of good trading opportunities out there at any given time, short term, long term, and everywhere in between.

Finding these opportunities is simply a matter of scrolling through price charts until the trade jumps out at you. You can also make use of many free services available through information providers.

BarChart provides a free service with a list of stocks at an all time high. These are perfect candidates for reversal trading. Reversal set ups are produced by extreme conditions.

Stock traders can begin with this list and pull up the charts on their favorite charting program. Interactive Brokers provides IB Options Brief. Stocks with unusual volatility or activity are good candidates for reversal trading.

Forex is the most volatile of all markets and there are many reversal opportunities in many time frames every day. Forex trades 24 hours a day 5 days a week. Many services are available online to alert you of market events.

I prefer to do my own research simply by viewing several charts until I discover a good trading set up. I also employ certain indicators to spot trading opportunities for me. I will share these various methods with you.

The recent popularity of online trading has provided the precarious advantage of "too much information". There is no way the trader can digest the amount of information available. There is no way to determine how reliable the information is. I personally ignore all this noise and stick to the charts except for a few sources that I will share with you.

Forex brokers are way ahead of stocks and commodities as far as charting and platform capabilities. It is comparatively easy to find what you're looking for on a forex charting platform. Many programs have been developed and tested for forex charting software. It is a good environment to sharpen your technical skills.

Futures traders can scroll through charts using the TracknTrade futures software. Most commodity contracts are available for download.

This particular chart is a perfect setup for a reversal trade. Price has risen quickly into major resistance and the trade volume has declined. This trade is setting up.

In order to initiate a low risk trade the stop loss must be set within the parameters of your money management plan. If the stop loss is set too close you risk getting stopped out of the trade. If it's too far away and the trade fails you risk losing more than your system allows.

Many novice traders find it hard to incorporate all the aspects of professional trading. I learned it the hard way, by losing money. If you follow the steps outlined in this brief publication you can start your trading journey the easy way, by learning from my mistakes.

You can practice these techniques trading for pennies, nickles, or dimes. I don't suggest trading on practice platforms with play money because the trade has no value and you may not take it seriously.

The Oanda forex platform provides no minimum deposit and you can trade with just enough money to make a loss uncomfortable. Their charting platform is intuitive and very easy to learn. Their order system is also easily navigated.

The trading principles outlined in this book apply equally to any market. Skills learned on the forex platform are easily adapted to stocks and commodities. Lessons learned with real money have a lasting effect.

Low risk trading is trading with money that you are able to lose. Your investment is game money. To stay in the game a rule based trading system is essential. The big players can anticipate your next move and shake you out.

The techniques covered provide more wins than losses but money management is still essential. It's easy to get carried away and bet the farm. I will cover all the aspects of money management in a later chapter.

High probability trading is making only trades that historically have a high success rate. In the Fibonacci chapter I will explain in detail the highest probability trade that I have discovered.

Avoid making trades based on the latest news. News is often leaked by the big players to initiate a response.

Jim Cramer explains how the Stock Market is Manipulated - YouTube
www.youtube.com/watch?v...
Jan 15, 2011 - 7 min - Uploaded by jorgepotter93jo
Click http://bit.ly/MakeMoneywithStocks Learn The Secret To Make Money whether the stock market is doing ...

Many investors trade only long positions. Learn to trade in both directions, long and short. If you don't have the margin necessary to make a short trade, buying a put option is an alternate method.

Wait for the trade to come to you. Don't jump in just to be in a trade. You can't lose your money if your not in the game and there is nothing wrong with sitting on the sidelines with cash. Patience is a virtue in the trading business.

If your capital is tied up in a bad trade you could miss a golden opportunity that comes your way. Don't settle for a mediocre set up while the best opportunity is coming your way. Wait for the best set-ups.

Due to high frequency trading, market manipulation is difficult to detect. Computer programs can enter large quantities of relatively small trades in a short period of time. This is trade based manipulation. They are creating an attractive market to trap the average investor.

The market will be rising, attracting some investors. At this point the big news will be leaked drawing in more and more investors through information based manipulation.

The price will spike up because of the great looking chart and the wonderful news. The program traders will now be selling while investors are still buying. They know that most investors will buy at the top and sell at the bottom.

Although we can't detect the program trading, just knowing the scenario gives us an edge in the marketplace. If we know what is going on we can control our losses by placing advanced orders to get us out of the market if the trade deteriorates.

Controlling losses is the highest priority of the professional trader. You should always enter a stop loss order when you open the position. Reversal trading enables us to set tighter stops than trend trading systems. Trend traders need to consider pullbacks and retracements.

The trend begins at the reversal point. Once in the trade you can run with the trend and adjust your stop loss for a risk free trade. The reversal trader becomes a trend trader. You can continue to reset the stop loss for a locked in profit while letting the trade run. If the market moves against you during the course of the trade the stop will be set for a locked in gain. Acceptable losses are the reality of trading. You will have losses. Controlling the amount of the loss is accomplished through technical analysis.

2 Analysis

Trading is the business of getting the odds in your favor. There is a fine line between trading and gambling. There are a few gambling ventures where you can get the odds in your favor but too few to mention.

The business of trading takes place before the trade is executed. All possible scenarios have been considered, win, lose, or draw. If the odds are in your favor and you apply good money management, you will be a successful trader.

Fundamental analysis requires a considerable amount of time. Analyzing the financial data of just one company is a time consuming process. From a technical point of view all this information is apparent on the price chart.

I place more emphasis on fundamental analysis when trading futures and forex. These are larger markets than stocks and the information is more difficult to manipulate. Many commodities are sensitive to the weather and I don't think they can manipulate the weather.....yet.

Commodities are traded worldwide on regulated exchanges such as the CME. Manipulation on futures contracts such as gold and oil require a great deal of money, however the big traders can still effectively move the price.

The currency (or Forex) market is the largest of all. Currencies are manipulated by countries through the central banks. China is not the only currency manipulator.

As far as the stock market is concerned there is no point

in doing fundamental analysis on thousands of stocks. Investors Business Daily will do it for you, for a nominal fee. They rate and rank stocks according to financial data. The time it would take the average investor to do this is not possible. If you are trading stocks it is well worth the few dollars they charge.

Google finance and Yahoo finance offer fundamental analysis free of charge. I refer to these on occasion but every time I do, it plants a bias in my head. A directional bias can be your worst enemy. It will sway your analysis and corrupt your technical skills. I try to avoid fundamental analysis on stocks and stick to the charts.

The big players have access to this information well in advance of me. In that respect, all the information is already on the chart. Much of this information can be manipulated to sway investors. The price chart is the only reliable source of current and historical information.

Major economic announcements can get the markets moving very quickly. You would be well advised to pay attention to this type of fundamental research. Recent and future announcements can be found on forexfactory.com. Some economic announcements can be major market movers.

The correlation of seemingly unrelated assets can be beneficial. If you are trading the stock market It is a good idea to watch the forex market, or at least the US dollar. All markets are related in some way. Normally when the Stock Market goes up, the Dollar goes down. If the dollar is going up, the market is probably going down. If the Stock market is flat and the dollar is going down, then gold is probably going up. The money doesn't go away, it just gets moved around.

We need to figure out where it is going next. and cash in on the move. This is easier said than done, but we can find clues. Here is an example.

The recent problems in Europe caused the EUR/USD pair to decline, meaning the Euro was declining in value while the US Dollar was going up in value. Meanwhile as the Dollar was advancing, the Stock Market was declining. This is business as usuall. The big players are moving money.

The DJ-30 just completed a Fibonacci retracement and the market is headed back up just in time for the annual Santa Clause Rally. This would be a good time for the EUR/USD to do a Fibonacci retracement so that the dollar declines, the stock market rallies, and all the players on Wall Street can enjoy the holidays with pockets full of money. You see, this is all just common sense, a game played by big players.

The US Dollar is a very significant indicator. All commodities worldwide must be paid for in US Dollars.

These three charts may illustrate the correlation of non related assets. Correlations can change over time.

These three charts indicate the big money has migrated from currency and gold to the stock market.

Seasonal charts are also useful as a reference and can be found on various websites including one of mine at fxharmonic.com. I refer to seasonality with currencies, indexes, commodities, and some stocks. I consider seasonality to be a flexible market force and it does not hold much weight in my decision to enter a short term position. It can be used for confirmation on a longer trade.

The dimensions of market analysis are fundamental and technical in nature. Traders analyze markets to determine the profit potential of an investment. The forces of supply and demand are under constant pressure from a variety of sources including social, economic and political events. The value of an asset can be studied in relationship to complex forces. The resulting analysis can be interpreted to provide an investment decision.

Even the best market analysis can fall short in its predictive ability. Probability and risk assessment are the objectives of market analysis in general with capital gain being the goal. Analysis techniques can be as diverse as the market being studied but some methods are commonly used. Equities, commodities, and many types of securities have market-specific fundamental aspects while technical analysis can be applied to all markets with a reasonable degree of predictability.

Fundamental analysis is the traditional method of market analysis. The factors involved depend on the general and specific markets being studied. The stock market is comprised of individual companies. The evaluation of corporate records can reveal past performance and the potential for future stability and growth.

Many commodities can be analyzed on a seasonal basis and some are sensitive to weather related events. The price of gold is related to the performance of other investments while the price of oil can be influenced by political events.

Fundamental analysis can be very complex because economic forces such as news releases, economic reports, and government intervention can drastically alter the expected outcome. There is no form of analysis that can incorporate unknown factors. Weather related events, war, and political disruption are systemic risk events. All investors are subject to systemic risk.

Technical methods involve the study of historical price charts in an effort to predict future asset values. Most technicians believe that fundamental aspects are incorporated on the price chart. Historical price charts are studied in various time frames from seconds to years.

Important patterns and price levels are detected that have proven results in the past. A myriad of formulas are available that might indicate the future direction of price. Indicators, patterns, and price levels are widely used in technical analysis. Trends, reversals, and more complex disciplines such as Fibonacci retracement and Elliot wave patterns are frequently used to detect market direction.

Macro analysis

It is beneficial for investors to analyze the "big picture" before making a final decision on an individual asset. When considering a stock purchase, the general market sentiment and volatility can be studied through fundamental and technical means.

Broad market indexes are examined in the same way individual assets are evaluated. Technical analysis is universal in nature because price charts for all assets are studied in a similar fashion. Fundamental values can be incorporated for large market segments such as the price/earnings ratio of the textile industry. Fundamental analysis is a time consuming process.

The economic conditions in other countries can exert forces on local markets. If the market as a whole is headed for a decline, a positive analysis of an individual asset may not be appropriate. Global markets influence commodity prices as well as local economic conditions.

Micro analysis

Broad markets can be segmented and classified according to common elements. The stock market is divided into sectors and industries. Sectors, such as transportation, can be divided into industries such as major airlines and railroads. The individual components are the companies within each industry.

Commodities are also divided into sectors like energy, which is composed of particular assets like ethanol, heating oil, or propane. Sectors, industries, and components can be analyzed using technical and fundamental methods.

Market analysis methods incorporate a broad spectrum of techniques that investors can use to make trading decisions. The purpose of analysis can be to determine the probability of a directional price movement.

Income producing investments can be analyzed to evaluate the stability of the company or asset. Commodities are evaluated to determine supply and demand issues. All methods are subject to interpretation.

Technical chart readers believe that all the fundamental analysis is incorporated on the chart. Major economic announcements would be the exception. Reports such as interest rate changes and the non-farm payroll report are market moving events.

I refer to the announcement schedule on Forexfactory.com. Entering a trade just prior to a major economic announcement would be considered a high risk trade unless your stop loss is set in stone. I normally avoid short term trading during these events.

3 Charting

Charting software is available in a wide variety of formats. Most brokers offer chart applications at no cost to account holders. Many of the free versions are as good or better than subscription and paid versions.

The trouble with charting software is the deluge of indicators. You could spend years amusing yourself with all the bells and whistles. I know because I did. At one point I had indicators indicating other indicators. This is madness.

Experimenting on these diverse indicators is counterproductive. Becoming an expert at reading a few indicators is very productive. All analysis and charting methods are subject to interpretation. To interpret chart studies you must be intimately familiar with the tools of the trade.

Ever changing market conditions distort chart readings. Unexpected volatility can create erratic market moves and it is sometimes difficult to detect manipulation. A picture is worth a thousand words and the price chart is a picture of what is going on.

I have used just about every charting software package out there. I stick to the basics and the free or broker supplied platforms are more than adequate. OptionXpress has a very flexible charting platform for stocks, options, and some futures contracts. They are a retail broker with retail prices but I like their charting platform.

Freecharts.com offers free commodity charts without technical drawing tools but free futures charts are hard to find. I use trackNtrade. There is a modest investment for the software and a recurring data feed expense. Charts without drawing tools are difficult to analyze.

Freestockcharts.com is a Worden Brothers product offering charting on stocks, forex, indexes, sectors, industries and many other market related charts. They offer a free version and a subscription version with scanning and sorting capabilities.

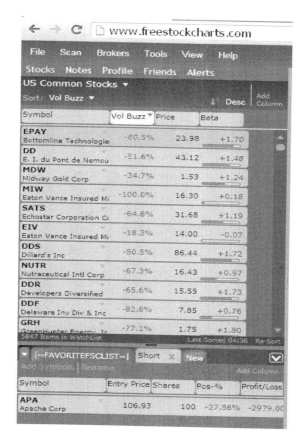

If you specialize in trading stocks, I would recommend the subscription version. Worden Brothers has the best stock analysis software available. The cost is very reasonable and the analysis tools are pretty good.

The free version does include free scans and limited sorting capability. The graphics are excellent and plenty of information on stocks is provided.

A fair amount of drawing tools are available and they are easy to use. Try scanning for new highs or lows for potential reversal candidates.

I began my trading using OHLC bars. At some point I switched to candles and have been there ever since. Candles offer an easier visual analysis than OHLC bars. I refer to candle wicks and doji candles. They can confirm a reversal.

Pay attention to the candle wicks. Long wicks can signal a reversal.

Open High Low Close (OHLC) is not as visual.

There is a lot of information out there about trading candle patterns but I prefer to stick to the very basic visual aids. I'm looking for reversal patterns and they are pretty easy to spot.

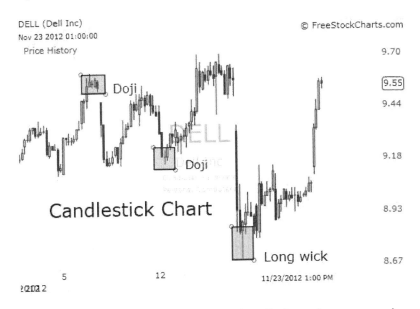

These simple patterns occur in all time frames and are useful to the day trader as well as the long term investor. There is something to be said for multiple time frame analysis. Start with longer time frames and work your way down.

Even the day trader should consult the daily, weekly, and monthly charts to gain an insight on the big picture. I usually begin my search on the daily charts. If I see an interesting set up I will view the weekly and monthly chart.

A trade entered on the daily charts will normally take weeks to develop. What kind of trade are you looking for? A trade using the 15 minute charts will probably take a day or two to run its course.

With a little practice these patterns will jump out at you. There is no need to memorize all the candle patterns or purchase recognition software. I specialize in reversal trading and a handful of chart patterns is all that is needed to find an opportunity.

Other chart patterns are useful and are fully explained online. I look for double tops and bottoms and head and shoulders patterns. They are relatively dependable reversal set ups. The more heavily traded assets tend to behave more consistently with chart patterns and indicators. Keep your trading simple.

I developed a day trading system years ago based on average candles. After years of research on the Amibroker charting platform, I found a common denominator to detect the big players entering the market. You can view this trading system on my website fx007.biz.

Since then Heiken-Ashi, or Average Candles were introduced and are similar in nature to my system and much easier to trade. Many tradable assets behave well with these candles and they are worth referring to.

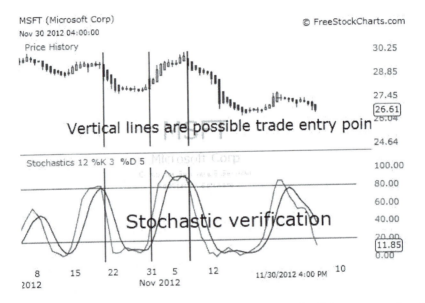

Never trade based on any single indicator or chart pattern. Always use multiple sources of signals and verification. When using patterns and indicators always have the support and resistance lines on the chart.

Trading is not an easy business. The concepts presented in this book may seem overwhelming to a new trader but with practice they will become second nature. The following chart shows a trade based on average candles.

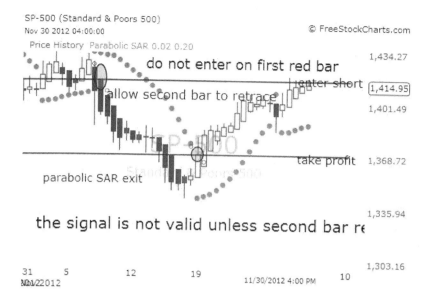

Reversals must be verified before entering the position. Allow the second bar to retrace the first bar by approximately one third before entering. Parabolic SAR normally provides a reasonable and safe exit.

Volume studies can be useful for determining the presence of big money in the game. It is best to view volume bars in a single color. Technically, for every buyer there must be a seller. On the average retail chart colored volume bars simply indicate if the bar closed up or down.

Most charting platforms have the ability to draw linear regression lines. I think that regression lines provide a more accurate analysis than trend lines and use them quite often. Regression lines can be applied to volume bars as well as price charts.

Volume studies are part of my analysis and I like to know if the big players are entering the market. As far as the stock market is concerned, the institutional traders enter the market at 2 or 3 pm, EST, when the bond market closes.

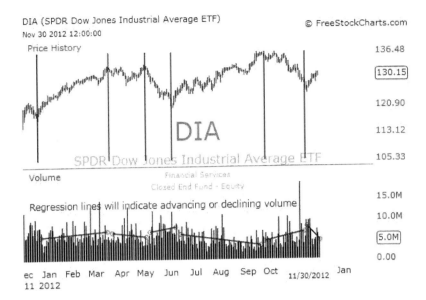

Volume spikes are big players. They buy when everyone is selling and sell when everyone is buying.

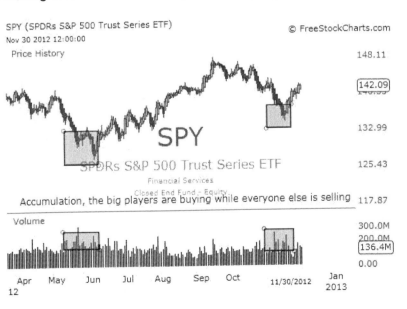

Accumulation, the big players are buying while everyone else is selling

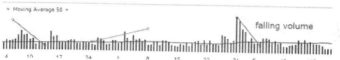

The above chart is a good example of a manipulated stock. Volume should rise with a rising market.

A few recurring chart patterns work well with reversal trading. Double tops and bottoms are reliable.

I don't actively search for these patterns but if I spot one it may initiate a trade.

4 Indicators

Most charting applications provide an abundance of indicators. Most are useless. It's not that the indicators have no value but most traders simply can't devote the time necessary to become adept at using them.

I was lost in the world of indicators for years, searching for the holy grail. My search is over. Success in trading is your own ability to develop a profitable system and stick to it.

I often refer to indicators to confirm my analysis of the price chart. MACD and STOCHASTICS have been around a long time and are reliable in ranging markets.

The vertical line confirms a Fibonacci pattern that produced the signal that initiated the trade. MACD 12,26,9 and stochastic 14,3,3 indicators confirm the trade signal. Don't try to make the indicator conform to your expectations

I use indicators for confirmation only. Divergence trading is the only exception.

The following chart illustrates a possible trade setup. Don't pick the fruit until it's ripe. Wait for a good setup.

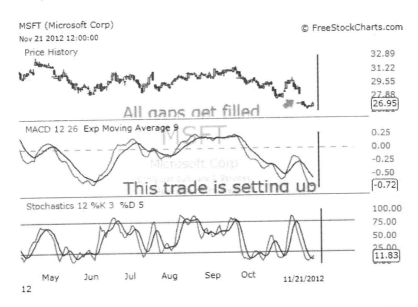

Notice the gap in the price chart. Price gaps get filled, sooner or later. This setup may or may not develop into a trade. Never chase a trade. Let it come to you.

If you fiddle with the indicators long enough, they will conform to your wishes. A preconceived bias is your worst enemy in trading. Watching the financial news and reading analyst opinions will put a bias in your head that is hard to get rid of.

When using these indicators, notice the past behavior in regard to the asset you are trading. Is it behaving correctly or is it jumpy and erratic. Oscillators work best in ranging markets. MACD and stochastics are oscillators and can become distorted in trending markets. If an indicator is historically inaccurate its predictive ability will have no future value.

Another indicator that I occasionally use in the actual trade is parabolic support and resistance. SAR is a fairly good exit strategy if you don't have time to monitor the trade. It will provide a safe exit but often leaves money on the table.

SAR has tendency to get you out of the trade a little early but there is nothing wrong with leaving money on the table. You will never get every dime out of a trade. Just hit the sweet spot and be grateful.

The above chart illustrates a Parabolic SAR exit. I have tried different settings but the original settings work the best. In this example, half the profit was left on the table but it is still a safe exit if you don't have time to monitor the trade.

You could also re-enter the trade on the pullback. This is the best exit indicator available and could be a trading system in itself. If using this as an entry, you will have to catch a long trend to become profitable. It does not work well in choppy markets.

Moving averages can be indicative, especially on larger time frames such as daily and weekly charts. I use the 20, 50, and 200 period simple moving averages. If price is above these averages it is considered very bullish. If below these it is very bearish. Various degrees are in between.

I would not initiate a trade based on moving averages (or any other indicator). They are an excellent reference when viewing the big picture.

Some day trading systems are based on pullbacks to the 20 period moving average but this system relies on a trend. The trend is your friend until the reversal occurs.

Day trading requires a great deal of time. A large investment is required to day trade stocks or futures. You can day trade for pennies in the forex market.

I would recommend Oanda for day trading the currency market. They have the lowest spreads, no minimum deposit, and a very fast execution platform. They also offer the MT-4 platform which is the best charting platform for market analysis.

The following chart is an example of a day trading method using the 20 period moving average.

Buy signals in blue box
5 minute scalping chart

Here is a image of the Oanda platform.

Five minute chart of the AUDCAD currency pair with a 20 period moving average. Notice how price bounces off the average during the trend.

Just as the actual price and the moving averages tend to merge together, the linear regression indicator acts in the same way. The following weekly price chart will illustrate the value of linear regression lines.

These are linear regression channels. The center line is the actual regression line. In the above example the daily and monthly regression line is just above the actual price. The weekly is lower, indicated by the purple squares.

If the price breaks upward through the daily and monthly regression line the downward trend may be over.

Daily linear regression chart of EURGBP. Current price is dead stop on the regression line.

The highest probability trade using indicators is the MACD divergence setup using double tops and bottoms.

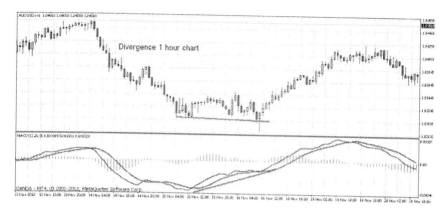

The chart above shows a double bottom on the price charts while the MACD indicator is rising. I use the canned settings of 12,26,9. I generally search for these patterns in the 15 minute time frame but they are valid in any time period. This is a high probability reversal trade.

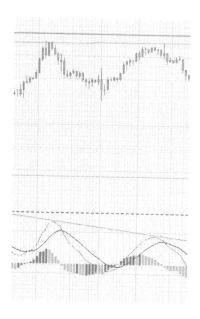

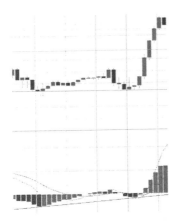

MACD divergence works well in double tops and bottoms but is also a valuable indicator for any reversal situation. The chart below shows price making a new high. The MACD indicator is falling and the price will soon follow. Divergence also works with stochastics but MACD has a greater probability. A tight stop loss can be used with this trade. It is a high probability, low risk trade

Divergence is a market anomaly. The chart is telling us that something is wrong. The following chart of volume divergence is a perfect example.

In the first rally the volume kept pace with the advancing price. In the second rally the volume was declining.

Volume analysis can enhance your general market perspective in all time frames.

The stochastic oscillator is can also be useful for divergence set ups.

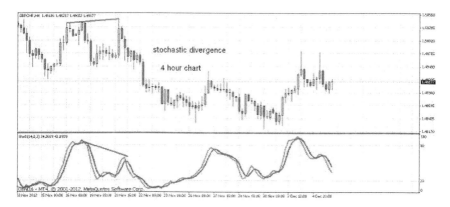

I run active searches for MACD divergence set ups and then check the stochastics for confirmation.

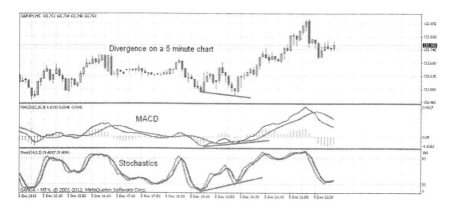

Divergence set ups are reliable high probability trades. Set your stop loss just beyond the extremes. Keep your profit / loss ratio at least 2:1. For one dollar at risk you expect to earn a two dollar profit.

These divergence trades are not hard to find. They occur every day in multiple markets and on multiple time frames. I prefer to scan for set ups in the 15 minute time frame. Win or lose, the trade will usually be completed the same day.

5 Trends
Support / Resistance

There is no charting application more powerful than support and resistance levels. Computer algorithms are set to respond to price fluctuations at certain price levels. These levels are prime targets for the reversal trader.

The following series of charts will illustrate just how far back in time these levels go.

This chart was randomly picked as I am writing this book on Thanksgiving day 2012. This is a forex chart of EURUSD.

The following chart was captured on the same charting platform as I scrolled back in time. The original resistance line has not been changed. You will be amazed at just how far back this price level has been effective. The shaded box highlights the areas at which the price bounced off this level.

This price level often acts as support or resistance.

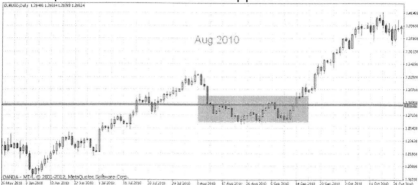

This is the same line as I scroll back through history.

At the risk of being redundant, I am trying to stress the importance of support and resistance levels.

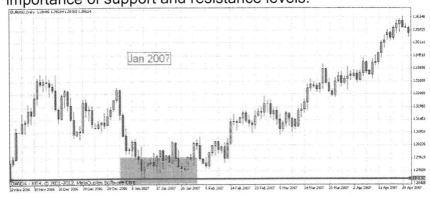

Hopefully, you get my point. These levels are essential in the reversal trading game. Of course, drawing trend lines from years back would be a tedious and time consuming project. Just do it the same way I did it.

Draw the horizontal line from the current price and scroll back to see if it is near reversal areas. Then strike another line from that key reversal area. Scroll forward and analyze your trade.

The MT-4 Metatrader platform offers many time saving algorithms for chart analysis. The following picture illustrates automatic support and resistance lines but they will not go back nearly as far as our previous study.

These lines can be initiated in any time frame. A link to download this indicator can be found on my website fxharmonic.com

Always put the higher timeframe levels on the chart, even if trading in a lower time frame. There is no need to place all the levels on your chart. Just insert the levels near the area you are trading. A monthly, weekly, or daily level is far more important than a 5 minute, 15 minute, or 1 hour time frame.

Trading a reversal near a support or resistance line is not a complicated matter. The following chart illustrates the entry and two possible exits. One exit for a winning trade and one exit for a losing trade.

If the analysis is incorrect, the trade will be exited with a small loss. It is imperative that you initiate your stop loss when placing the trade. Do not place the stop loss too close to the S/R (support/resistance) line. This is a judgment call and depends on your risk appetite, money management plan, and analysis of previous attempts of price to break through this line.

There are many possible exit strategies. If you monitor the trade often, you may not want to initiate a take profit order. If you prefer to set it and forget it there are a few possibilities.
- Set the exit at the nearest support level.
- Set the exit at a fibonacci retracement level.
- Set the exit on a trend line estimate.

If the trade goes bad, you should be out soon with a reasonable loss. If the trade goes well, the stop loss can be reset to lock in a profit. At this point you could let the trade run as long as possible if it maintains profitability. I prefer the stress free "set it and forget it" method of trading.

Trend lines can be traded or used for entry and exit strategies. Always draw a rising trend line below the price and a falling trend line above the price. The MT-4 platform provides an automatic trend line tool that works very well. Multiple time frame trends can be displayed on the same page. The following chart illustrates this excellent charting tool.

A link to download this tool can be found on my website fxharmonic.com. All of my websites are free to use. Combine trend lines with support and resistance levels to get a clear picture of whats going on.

6 Fibonacci

Fibonacci retracements occur in all markets and in all time frames, all of the time. This would suggest that the trader using Fibonacci drawing tools should easily be able to profit on all trades. Unfortunately, this is not the case.

A successful Fibo trade requires the timing of a reversal. Timing when the retracement will begin is the tricky part. One timing technique has been developed and has been tested to provide better than 70% accuracy.

Fibonacci was a twelfth century mathematician responsible for spreading the arabic numeral system we use today. The Fibonacci sequence of numbers relates to the golden ratio of 1.618. The fibo ratios we use in charting applications are directly related to his research.

Using a trading system with a 70% win ratio simply requires a risk aversion system of cutting the 30% losses short. Reversal trading allows you to set up trades with a minimum of 2:1 profit : loss ratio.

With the odds on your side, you can have a profitable trading system if you follow the rules on every trade. The money management plan is essential. Trade confirmation is equally important. Never rush into a trade. Wait for the set up to develop.

Every charting platform provides Fibonacci drawing tools and every chart you pull up will have a fibo retracement on it. All of these patterns are not good trading candidates for a variety of factors.

These charts show how precise Fibonacci levels are.

Fibonacci retracements are valid in all time frames, from seconds to months. This monthly chart goes back to 1999.

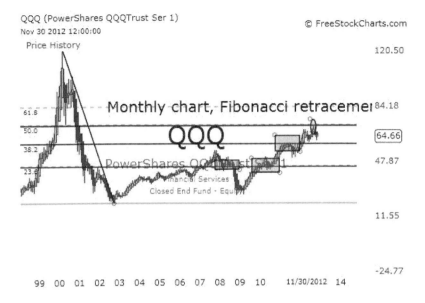

No one knows why fibo numbers work. Is it a cosmic force of nature or a self fulfilling prophecy ? The answer to that question doesn't matter to me. It just works and I use it.

Combining Fibonacci retracements with chart patterns has recently attracted a lot of research. As early as 1935 a man named H.M. Gartley published a book called "Profits in the Stock Market". He discovered a reversal pattern that is still being used today.

Larry Pesavento further developed this pattern recognition system and Scott Carney continued the research. Eugeni Neumoin wrote a program to automate the indicator on the Metatrader charting platform. It has been further developed and refined over the years. It is called the ZUP indicator, Universal Zig Zag with Pesavento Patterns. A link to this indicator can be found on my website fxharmonic.com.

The ZUP indicator is an amazing piece of work. Combined with the other trading concepts outlined in this book, a very profitable trading system can be developed. The ZUP indicator can be applied in any time frame making it suitable for day trading, long term investing, and swing trading.

To examine an article written by the creator of the ZUP indicator go to "articles.mql4.com/444".

Trading the ZUP indicator is not quite as simple as it appears. I have spent a great deal of time studying this indicator. As with all indicators you need to know how to read it. All indicators are subject to interpretation. I will show you how to trade it in the final chapter of this book.

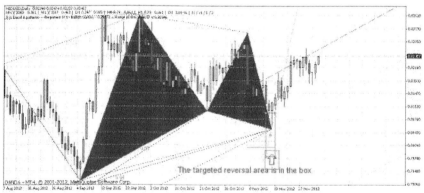

The above chart shows the ZUP indicator on a daily forex chart. All of the lines you see are Fibonacci ratios from many reversal areas. Certain combinations of ratios provide the most probable conditions for a reversal trade. The pattern lights up when these conditions occur.

Some patterns work better than others and some fail. The win ratio is better than 70% and this is no easy accomplishment in the technical trading arena. I will cover many of the nuances of this fascinating indicator.

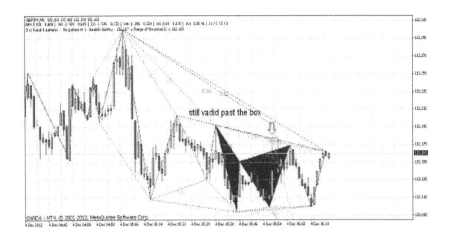

These charts show the ZUP indicator on one and five minute charts. Notice how the indicator was still valid after the box on the one minute chart above. Below is a five minute chart. It took me three minutes to find these charts as I am writing. Far too many opportunities are available every day. These are excellent day trading opportunuties. The ZUP indicator is a high probability, low risk trade set up.

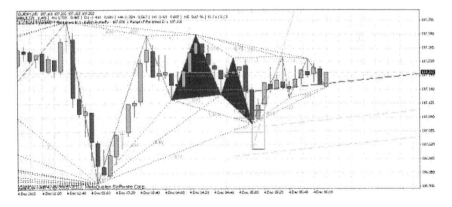

I have personally seen very few failures, less than the ratio I have stated. In all fairness to the reader, I would rather err on the side of caution.

The ZUP indicator is also a valuable tool for the long term investor. Here is a weekly forex chart.

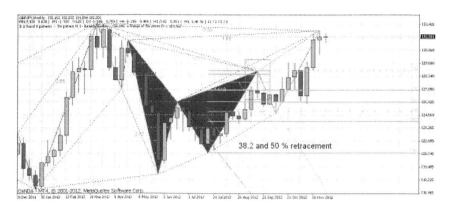

This set up was good for a Fibonacci retracement. I would consider all reversals to be a retracement until proven otherwise. I am going to say it again, because it is important. Consider all reversals to be a retracement until the retracement line is broken and verified.

This should be a major consideration when planning to exit a profitable trade. The targeted win should also be considered when setting the stop loss. You would never risk two dollars to win one dollar. You must know your exits before entering a trade. If the numbers don't work, don't make the trade.

When viewing the chart you have to work the numbers to see if risk and reward numbers are acceptable. Your money management plan will tell you how much you can lose per trade. The acceptable loss will determine the amount you can trade for.

If you do not adhere to your own trading rules you will lose money. If you do not apply the rules to every trade you will lose money. There are many ways to lose, and only one way to win.

I will provide more examples of the ZUP indicator. The MT-4 trading platform is set up mainly for forex but it can also be used to research some stocks and commodities. In the United States you can not trade stocks from the MT-4 platform but you can use it for research.

Other countries offer trading on CFDs which are derivatives called contracts for difference. CFDs on stocks and indexes mirror the movement of the actual asset. These derivative are tradable in most countries excluding the USA.

Residents of the USA are not permitted to trade on these platforms. As far as I know, it is legal to open a practice account with these brokers for research purposes. That is how I can utilize the ZUP indicator on stocks and commodities. I simply trade them with regulated US brokers.

Most of the stocks available are heavily traded stocks which are the safest stocks to trade. Options can also be traded on these assets and that will be the subject of a later publication. I rarely do my research on the same platform that I trade on. Some are better for research and others are better for trading.

Interactive Brokers is possibly the best platform for stocks and options but their charting leaves a lot to be desired. The MT-4 platforms offers the best technical research. The Oanda platform offers the ability to enter your stop loss and take profit order when you enter the trade.

Oanda is the easiest platform to trade forex. It is very fast and the drawing tools are easy to use but you can't get the ZUP indicator on it. Researching on one platform and trading on another is the way I work. It is not that hard to do and remember, we are never in a hurry to enter a trade. Most of my reasearch is conducted on the MT-4 software.

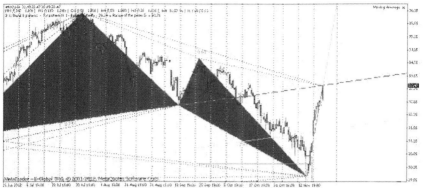
Daily stock chart of MO with the ZUP indicator above.

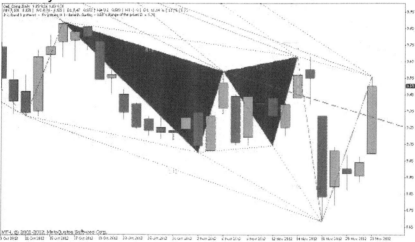
ZUP indicator forecasting DELL collapse above.

I have rarely seen this indicator fail but the entry is a little tricky. The box provided by the creator is the expected reversal area. Many times the price will go beyond or above this box and still remain valid.

This is why I never rush into a trade. These signals occur many times each day in all time frames. There are way too many opportunities to enter a trade so take your time and select the best possibility. Choose the time frame based on your expected "take profit" horizon.

The above chart is a 5 minute time frame suitable for day trading. The entry is confirmed by stochastics.

This potential trade may develop. Wait for confirmation.

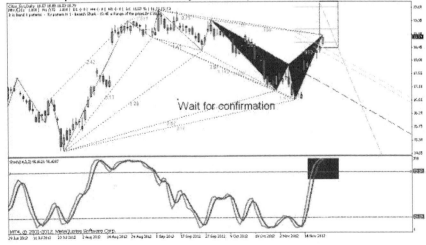

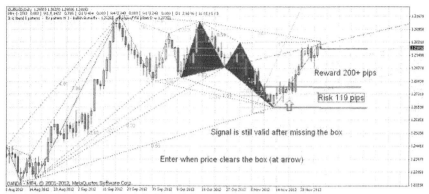
Trading is about risk and reward.

Plan your 2 exits before entering a position, win or lose.

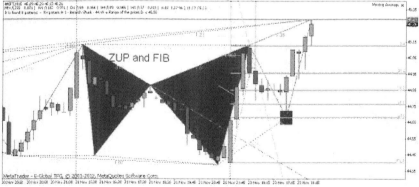
Consider all reversals to be a retracement until proven otherwise. This provides a reasonable profit and the take profit order can be placed when you enter the trade. Don't be greedy. Take a modest profit and get out before the sharks eat you.

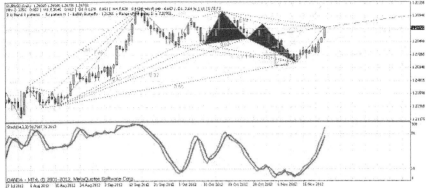

Another form of confirmation is essential.

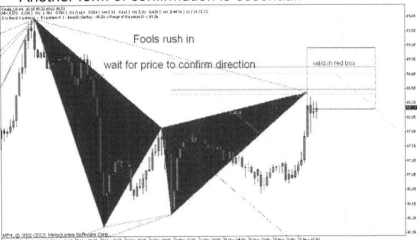

Fools rush in. Let the set up develop.

15 minute chart of AIG is good for a fibo retracement.

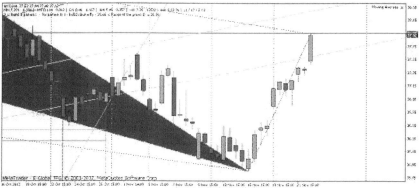
KO ran away and never looked back.

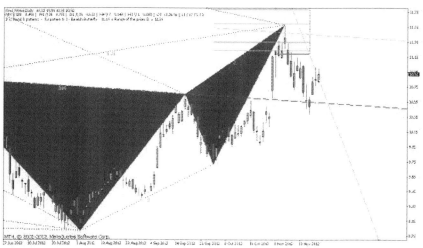
This is a retracement for Ford and the upward trend will probably continue.

Reversal trading incorporates major trend reversals, pullbacks, Fibonacci retracements, and market corrections. The best method to determine the nature of the reversal is the use of support, resistance, and trend lines. If you don't do your homework before you trade, you will lose money.

There are many ways to lose money in the trading game and few ways to make money. This book describes one way.

7 Orders

Novice traders can incur losses because they don't know exactly how to make the trade. Orders can be confusing.

BASIC TERMS WE USE :

When you BUY a stock, you are <u>opening</u> a LONG position (you think it will go up)

When you SELL(short) a stock, you are <u>opening</u> a SHORT position (you think it will go down)

When you BUY a stock that you have sold SHORT, you are <u>closing</u> a short position.(cover)

When you SELL a stock that you own, you are <u>closing</u> a long position.

No matter what trade you make, you are OPENING a position or CLOSING a position.
(other than adding to or subtracting from an existing position)

You can open a position LONG or SHORT.

You can close an open position.

These basic terms apply to stocks, options, and forex.

Don't start pushing buttons unless you fully understand the implications.

BASIC ORDERS YOU NEED TO KNOW:

MARKET order (buy or sell it RIGHT NOW , I don't care what price it is.)

LIMIT order (buy or sell it as soon as possible, at $XXX or better)

You tell them what you are willing to pay or what you are willing to sell for.

This type of order may not get FILLED , the price must remain beyond your limit until the order is filled.

STOP order (when the price hits $XXX, turn my order into a MARKET ORDER.

STOP LIMIT order (when the price hits $XXX, turn my order into a LIMIT ORDER.

A DAY ORDER is good for the day. This order will either be FILLED or canceled at the end of the trading day.

A GOOD TILL CANCELED order will either be FILLED or remain valid until you cancel it.

These are all the BASIC ORDERS you need to know. There are other types of orders for advanced players. You don't need them to trade profitably.

A good broker will fill your order AT or BETTER than what you asked for.

Be careful what you ask for. You just might get it.

ORDER WHAT YOU WANT:

what you want:
XYZ stock has been coming down for weeks and is currently trading at $10 . You think its a good deal, but you don't want to pay more than $10 for it. It doesn't matter if you get filled today, as long as you get it for $10 or less.
You want to open a long position for 100 shares at $10 or less as soon as possible.
what to order:
Stock ticker: XYZ
Amt: 100
Type of order: BUY LIMIT
Limit price: $10
Good till Canceled

what you want:
Same as above, only $10 or so is close enough, and you want it right now.
what to order:
Type of order: BUY MARKET
Day Order

what you want:
Same as above, only you think it will go lower. You wont pay more than $9 for it. But its now or never.
what to order:
Type of order: BUY STOP LIMIT
Stop Limit Price: $9
Day Order

what you want:
Same as above, only $9 or so is close enough and there is no hurry.

what to order:
Type of order: BUY STOP
Stop price: $9
Good till Canceled

THE MORE STRICT YOUR ORDER - THE LESS CHANCE IT WILL BE FILLED.

ORDER WHAT YOU NEED:

You own 100 shares of XYZ stock. You paid $10 per share. You want to sell it.
You want to SELL TO CLOSE your position.

what you want:
Your stock is currently trading at $15. You want out right now for around a $5 profit.
what to order:
Type of order: SELL MARKET
Amt: 100
Day Order

what you want:
Your stock is trading at $15, but you think it will go to $16 and you will not sell for less than $16. No big hurry.
what to order:
Type of order: SELL STOP LIMIT
Stop Limit price: $16
Good till canceled

what you want:
Your stock is trading at $15. You have placed a sell stop limit to sell at $16. The market is volatile and the price may drop back to $10. You want to make at least $3 per share on this trade, more or less, and you want to protect this profit if the price drops.

what to order:
Type of order: SELL STOP (also referred to as a STOP LOSS)
Sell Stop price: $13
Good till Canceled

YOU ARE NOT CHARGED FOR AN ORDER UNLESS THE ORDER IS EXECUTED.

JUST IN CASE ORDERS:

what you want:
You have been watching XYZ stock for awhile. You don't have time to watch the market during the week. It's trading at $10 and you are willing to pay $8 or less.

what to order:
Ticker: XYZ
Amt: 100
Type of order: BUY STOP LIMIT
Buy Stop Price: $8
Good till Canceled

what you want:
You own XYZ stock. You paid $10. You don't have time to watch the market, but just in case the market spikes up to $15, you'll take it. Anywhere near that price is a great profit.

what to order:
Ticker:XYZ
Amt:100
Type of order: SELL STOP
Sell stop price: $15
Good till Canceled

Make sure your broker is using the same terminology that I am using here. Some brokers differ slightly. DONT MAKE A TRADE UNLESS YOU KNOW WHAT YOU ARE DOING.

You can issue as many orders as you like as long as your account is funded well enough to cover them.

I hope that I have provided enough examples. These combinations can go on and on. Your orders depend on your circumstances. On the Oanda FOREX platform you can enter a STOP LOSS order and a TAKE PROFIT order at the same time you place your buy or sell order. Their TAKE PROFIT is the same as a STOP or STOP LIMIT order. So watch your brokers terminology, and write it down so you remember.

OptionsXpress order ticket

Stock	Extended Hours	Trailing Stop	Contingent
Stock Symbol	AKS	Find Symbol	
Action	Buy		
Quantity	100	○ Shares ○ $ Amount All or None ☐	
Price	○ Market		
	○ Limit $ 13.50		
	○ Stop $ 13.50		
	● Stop Limit		
	○ Market On Close		
Duration	Good Until Cancelled		
Routing	Default		
Advanced Orders	None		
	Preview Order		Save

Oanda Forex order ticket

MT-4 order ticket

FXCM trade on chart

or from dealing rates

8 Money Management

<u>Your money is at risk if you have an open position in the market.</u>

Do not trade without a Money Management Plan and a Trade Management Plan. Always keep in mind that if some terrible event occurs, such as 911, the entire market could crash and you may lose ALL of your money. This is called SYSTEMIC RISK, and it is the risk that every participant in the market assumes, whether they want to or not.
Well, that's the bad news. The good news is that you can control the amount of risk that you are willing to assume.

RISK and REWARD go hand in hand. The more risk you are willing to assume, the more profit or loss you will take. This is just common sense. However , there are skills that you can learn that will lower your risk.

If we utilize a money management plan and place our trades carefully, we may be able to tip the scales in our favor.

A money management plan is very easy to set up. It is based on HOW MUCH WE CAN LOSE. Everyone wants to know how much they can make. Well, the answer is the sky is the limit.

If I ask you how much you can lose, the answer will not be the sky is the limit. This is exactly the question you should be asking yourself. How much am I willing to lose?

This is why we are constantly preaching DO NOT TRADE WITH MONEY YOU CANT AFFORD TO LOSE. If you want to gamble, go to Vegas. It's more fun than trading.

The easiest way for me to explain how to set up your money management plan is by example.

Stock Market example:

Let's say that you have a $2000 trading account for trading stocks. You are just learning to trade and you are prepared for some losses(even the best pro's have losses).

With $2000, you want to open a MARGIN account. You will have to come up with half the cost of a stock purchase. Your broker will lend you the rest. This will allow you to look at stocks priced up to $20 per share or so. So now, your universe of stocks may be SP-500 stocks priced under $20.

The question is how much can you trade for and how much can you lose on each trade.

My general rule is "risk no more than 5% of the account value on each trade" so we will use this for our example. 5% of $2000 is $100. So we can't lose more than $100 per trade.

You decide to buy 100 shares of AK Steel @ $15 per share. You need to place a STOP LOSS order at $14 per share. $1 times 100 shares = $100 loss. That is a pretty tight stop loss unless AKS is sitting on a major SUPPORT line.

Maybe it would be better to buy Dryships. DRYS is trading at $5 per share. We need to place our SELL STOP at $4. This is a wide stop, and gives us plenty of breathing room. If DRYS is sitting on SUPPORT we may decide to place our STOP LOSS at $4.50, giving us a $50 loss if the trade goes bad.

The general idea here is to know how much you can lose BEFORE entering a trade. If you are willing to lose 10% of your account value on each trade, then adjust the formula accordingly.

Combine your money management with the laws of support and resistance. And here is a tip: don't place your stop too close to the support line. The Market Makers may drop the price just below the line to TAKE OUT the traders before running the price up.

These examples are based on the assumption that you are not a long term buy and hold investor. If you are buying stocks to hold and collect dividends, a stop loss order may not be appropriate.

Most stocks will eventually turn profitable sooner or later. The market has been going up since 1920. The two exceptions are the tech bubble of 2000 and 911. These are systemic events and the risk involved is known as systemic risk.

Stop loss orders are appropriate for swing traders and other short term traders. Stop loss orders are always appropriate in the forex market.

FOREX example:

Lets say you have a $1000 forex account. Margin on forex can be as high as 50 to 1, allowing you to trade for $5 per pip. But do you really want to ? Lets figure it out.

Using my 5% rule, we could withstand a $50 loss on each trade. If we are trading for $5 per pip, that would give us a 10 pip stop loss. I can tell you from experience, that is not enough. The optimal stop loss for EUR/USD is 36 pips. The maximum I would trade for with a $1000 account is for $1 per pip.

Forex is the most volatile of all markets. You will incur many losses with tight stop losses.

SUPPORT,RESISTANCE, and FIBONACCI retracements are of utmost importance when trading forex. Economic announcements will create volatile conditions. You should not be in the market during these announcements unless you are prepared to accept the risk. Refer to Forexfactory.com for these announcements.

Of all the economic announcements, the Non-farm payroll report creates the most volatility. This announcement is released on the first Friday of each month at 8:30 AM EST.

In conclusion:
I don't know how much money you can make trading the markets. If you do not know how to place an order, you will lose money. If you do not manage your risk, you will lose money. There are many ways to lose money in the markets. Don't make stupid mistakes with incorrect orders or trading with too much at risk.

All trading systems, including day trading systems, must have three basic components. These components are Money Management, Risk Management, and Trading Rules. Many trading accounts have been wiped out due to a poor or even no money management plan.

Many novice traders concern themselves with how much money they can make when they should be concerned with how much money they can lose. To begin with, the trading account itself should be comprised of risk capital. Beyond that, an acceptable loss per trade must be determined.

A good rule of thumb may be 3% to 5% of total account value may a reasonable loss per trade. For example, with an account size of $2000, an acceptable loss per trade would be 5% or $100. With a maximum loss per trade of $100 we can now determine which securities, options, or currencies we are able to trade.

We could purchase an option contract for $100 or less. We could also trade forex for $5 per pip with a 20 pip stop loss in place. The money management plan can be applied to any market. Just do the math.

The next component of the trading system is Risk Management. Part of the risk management plan has already been determined. We will lose a maximum of $100 per trade. There are two ways to accomplish this.

The first is to sit in front of the computer and watch the screen as the trade develops with your finger on the exit button. The other, and much easier on the nerves way, is to initiate a stop loss when the position is opened. This "set it and forget it" method takes all the emotion off the table. The only reason to watch a trade progress is to manage an early exit to cut losses or profits. If you have developed a sound system, there is no need to cut out early.

The third component of the trading system is the actual trading rules. Systems can be automated or manual, in other words you can visibly see the trade signals develop on the chart or you can set up a software program to do it for you.

Most systems do not work at any time of day or during economic announcements. So unless you can program these events into your system, it may be best to manually trade the system. Most trading systems have been developed through the use of back testing.

A system can be based on price action, indicators, and chart patterns. To develop a sound trading system you will need software with back testing capabilities. Amibroker is one of the least expensive development platforms available at under $300, and comes with free intraday forex data.

Many other platforms are available and can be found with a simple web search. Your system will need an entry signal and two exit signals. One exit will be for a profitable trade and the other exit will be for a losing trade. The exit strategy must be formulated before entering the trade. The profit potential and maximum loss must be set before entering the trade.

After extensive back testing has been done, you should have a probability of wins and losses which can be stated in a ratio such as 1:2 meaning one out of two trades is a winner or 50%. You should also have a Risk/Reward or profit and loss ratio such as 2:1 meaning the system will risk one dollar to make two dollars.

Then you put it all together and you may have a system that wins two dollars and loses one dollar 50% of the time. If you can develop a system such as this you will be a wealthy trader in no time at all. It is easier said than done.

The point is, before trading, work the numbers. Know how much you can win and how much you can lose. Are the odds in your favor ?

Option trading can be used in risk aversion tactics. This will be the subject of my next book, but I would like to share a few words about trading derivatives.

The term "complex derivatives" in mathematics refers to the complex analysis of variables. In the context of financial markets, complex derivatives are contracts in which the price is derived from an underlying asset. All financial derivatives are complex. The complexity depends on the contract terms and the underlying asset. The underlying asset may itself be a derivative.

Underlying assets may include stocks, indexes, currencies, and commodities. The value of the derivative contract depends on the price of the asset and the terms of the contract. Derivative contracts can be futures contracts, options, and swaps among others.

The price of a derivative is related to the future price of the underlying asset. The contract terms include a price and an expiration date. Derivatives are highly leveraged instruments. Trading complex derivatives requires a great deal of knowledge about the underlying asset being traded. A full understanding of how derivatives work is essential.

Futures contracts are complex derivatives. The underlying assets are usually commodities such as agricultural or precious metal products. Many other types of commodities are underlying assets for futures contracts. These contracts are traded on the open market through organized and supervised exchanges.

Option contracts may be the most commonly traded derivative. Options are available on nearly every tradable asset. The most common option contracts include an underlying asset, a strike price, and an expiration date. The option contract will increase or decrease in value depending on the value of the asset on or before expiration. Other factors are involved in option pricing.

Specific formulas are used when pricing these complex derivatives. Volatility of the underlying asset and current interest rates are two of the variables used in pricing options. Options can be traded in combinations. These combined option trades are referred to as strategies. Option strategies can be very complex derivatives.

Options are also available on futures contracts. This type of trade would be a derivative of a derivative. Both contracts have an expiration date. The futures contract would have a physical underlying asset. The underlying asset for the options contract would be the futures contract. These complex derivatives can be quite intricate.

Some complex derivatives are traded on the over the counter market. These contracts are simply an agreement between two parties. The over the counter market is unregulated these contracts are not exchange traded contracts. Even though complex derivatives are considered to be highly risky, trading on an exchange may provide some risk aversion.

In today's volatile marketplace risk aversion tactics are of utmost importance. Before you trade, know the risk involved and have a plan to avoid as much risk as possible.

Option trading will be the subject of my next book.

9 Make the Trade

Technical analysis works equally well for any tradable asset. The technical trader is able to control multiple trading accounts with specialized brokers. I trade stocks, options, futures, and forex. There is a trade set up waiting for me at any given time, day or night.

This flexibility in asset classes provides numerous trading opportunities. I maintain multiple accounts for trading and research purposes. For example, I trade forex on the Oanda trading platform but do most of my research on the Metatrader MT-4 platform. Interactive Brokers has the most attractive commission rates but OptionsXpress has a better charting platform.

You need to have a funded account to have access to the best research brokers but the cost is comparatively minor. My money management rules apply to each trading account individually. The maximum loss I am willing to accept is 5% of the account value and normally much less.

For a $5,000 dollar forex trading account I am willing to lose a maximum of $250 per trade. For a $2,000 stock and options account I would be willing to risk $100 per trade. Work the numbers and decide on your own appetite for risk.

Trade confidence plays a role in the risk I am willing to assume. If I am highly confident I will risk the 5%. If I am moderately confident I may be willing to assume a 3% loss.

Your trading style should suit your personality. Day trading is exciting but watching a trade in progress can be a stressful experience. I enjoy day trading on occasion but I am too laid back to make a habit of it.

I prefer the "set it and forget it" style of trading. I am just not into staring at computer screens all day. I set my trades and go about my daily lifestyle. To do this you must have a good trading system and a money management plan. When I enter a position I know all the possible outcomes.

For example, my position on XYZ company will have 3 possible outcomes when I return to my trading desk. I will have a profit of $200 or a loss of $100 or the trade will still be in progress. It's just that simple. There is no stress because I can afford to lose $100 and a profit of $200 is reasonable and acceptable.

I have done my homework so the odds are in my favor for a winning trade. I know the market can be unpredictable and I am willing to accept a loss. Trading is not rocket science but it does require a modest investment in time.

You also must determine the time frames you are interested in trading. Most of my trading would be considered swing trading. I like the trade to be over in less than one week and preferably a day or two. I think day trading is stressful and I don't have the patience for long term investing.

You must decide which style is most comfortable for you. Trading should be fun and not a stressful chore. I trade the 15 minute, 1 hour, and 4 hour charts. I never make a trade without referring to the daily, weekly, and monthly charts. The most important support and resistance levels are on the longer time frames. This is also true with trend lines. Draw the lines on the big charts then drop back down to the time frame you are trading.

You need to choose one or more trading strategies. The strategy requires a signal or pattern that you will be searching for. My favorite is the ZUP indicator and I will enter trades based on this signal if confirmed. Setting up a scan for this signal is relatively easy on the MT-4 platform.

If you are not trading with a broker that uses this platform then just download a free practice account from any of a number of brokers. Then download and install the ZUP_v102.mq4 version of this indicator. Make sure you get the v102 version because some of the others do not work well. You can get it is here:
http://www.forex-tsd.com/harmonic-trading/885-price-patterns-gartley-butterfly-bat-135.html
Or go to my website fxharmonic.com where I have posted a link.

Download this indicator into MT-4/experts/indicators. Now pull up a chart and double click the custom indicator and save it as a template. Now you can scan through your charts in different time frames. You will be amazed at how many signals you will get. There are too many to trade and some are not good trade set ups.

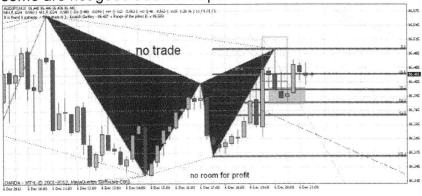

The above chart shows a valid signal but there is not enough room for profit on a retracement. You are looking for a 2:1 profit / loss ratio.

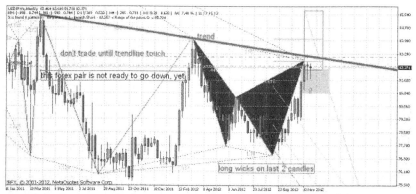

This forex pair is a set up in progress. I would not enter this trade until price touches the trend line. Take your time and select only the best set ups.

This set up jumped right out of the box and retraced on the next bar. The opportunity is over.

As you can see, all signals are not good candidates for a variety of reasons. If you can't find a really great set up then don't trade at all. Try again later.

In my earlier trading days I would take any set up that came down the road just for the sake of trading. The smart trader is like a predator, patiently waiting for the precise moment to attack. Timing is everything in the trading game. Wait for the big players to show their cards before placing a bet. The only advantage we have is flexibility and speed.

This is a very nice set up. The first candle in the box

spiked down and closed dead on support with a long tail. Notice how price has been trending up and the retracement has already occurred, You could stay in this trade and ride the trend. Move your stop loss up to lock in a profit.

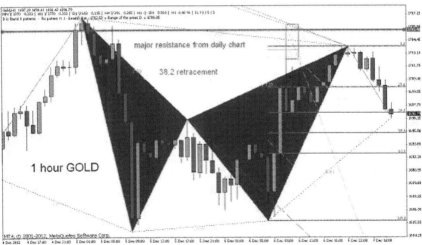

Notice how price has gone beyond the box. The signal is still valid and you will see this quite often. It does not pay to jump in too quickly. Price stopped dead on the 38.2 Fibonacci retracement. I would have entered this trade on the doji candle.

I have pulled every chart in this book up as I was writing the book. They are all common everyday set ups.

This is a long term trade from a weekly chart. I bought a call option on Microsoft a few months out. I don't normally look for long term trades but if I see a good set up I will trade options on it.

Kraft is at an all time high based on the monthly chart. This is a one hour chart. The ZUP pattern is a little distorted but I think this is a tradable set up.

There is a fine line between system trading and discretionary trading. All set ups are subject to interpretation. When trading the stock market, the expected direction of the broad market index will play a large part in my decision.

Most stocks will keep pace with the larger indexes such as the SP-500. It is also beneficial to track the industry or sector to see if the big money is coming or going.

This is a great set up. The ZUP indicator plus a triple bottom. Notice the long tail on the candle as it bounced off support. This is an easy retracement trade with a perfect stop loss placement just below support.

I could go on and on with examples. For more trading examples go to my website fxharmonic.com. All of my websites are free and contain information not covered in this publication. My home website is Lakeside21.com.

I hope you have gained a few nuggets of wisdom from this book. The ZUP indicator is working for me but you need to find what works for you. The other trading principles discussed in this book are basic technical skills used by professional traders.

I wish you the best in your trading adventures. Make money, have fun, and don't get stressed out. It's just a game.

STOCHASTIC FULL
12, 3 5
LINEAR REGRESSION LINES?